1

Knowledge Books and Software

A long time ago, the land went out where the ocean is today. There was a beautiful forest of gum trees, banksias and wattles. The old gums were so large, you could not reach your arms around them.

Knowledge Books and Software

3

The she-oaks whispered in the wind. The golden wattles had a yummy gum. Wallabies, wombats and echidnas lived nearby. Colourful birds lived in the trees. Frogs and snakes lived near the creeks. It was a land of plenty.

4

Knowledge Books and Software

An angry giant owned this land. He did not allow anyone else to hunt or gather from his country. He listened to the willy wagtail who told him of strangers on his land.

Knowledge Books and Software

7

One hot summer's day, the giant was walking through his country. He saw some women with their grass baskets full of gum. In an angry rage, he cried, "Who is stealing my gum?" The women begged him to forgive them but he would not listen. He had not seen that his two wives were also there.

Knowledge Books and Software

9

The giant became even more angry. He sat on the grass in a very bad mood. He then called on the Southern Ocean to come in and drown the women.

Knowledge Books and Software

11

Knowledge Books and Software

The wind changed. The sky grew dark and stormy. The cold, green sea became rough. The waves rushed in to drown the women. That night, a high tide and full moon kept the forest flooded. Salt water covered much of the land, never to return.

Knowledge Books and Software

13

The giant was very sad now. He had drowned his two wives. He had lost his grasslands in the south. He had drowned his forest and ruined his best hunting grounds.

Knowledge Books and Software

Ngaram

15

Over the years, the old, giant trees fell into the deep water. They are now turned to stone, flint and rocks. They lay like sunken treasure chests at the bottom of the ocean.

Knowledge Books and Software

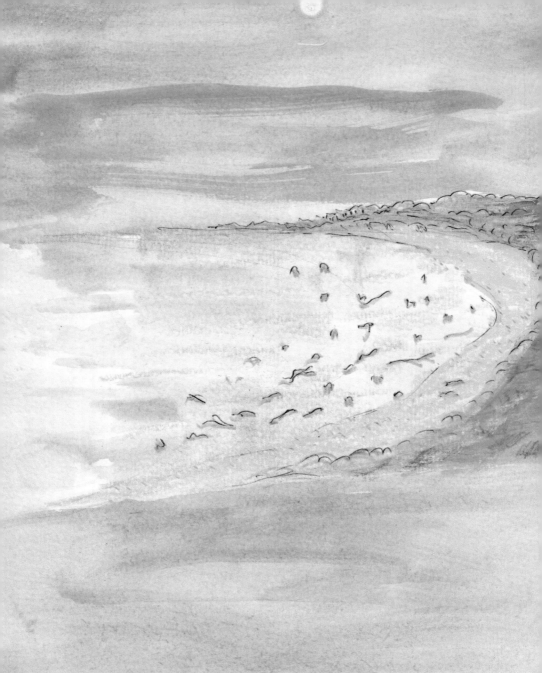

17

The parrots are now the parrotfish. Echidnas are now the spiky crayfish hiding under ledges. Wedge tail eagle is now the big, black stingray. Brown snake is now the conger eel. The ghosts are now the octopuses.

Knowledge Books and Software

19

The giant lived a long and lonely life, looking out to sea at his sunken forest of dreams. He listened to his wives calling for help in the cold, green water. They are now the sea lions that swim among the kelp forests and fallen tree branches. They are forever looking for wattle gum to please him.

Knowledge Books and Software

21

The sea stayed where it is right to this very day. On a starry night, if you look closely, you can still see the sunken spirits dancing in the shallows.

Knowledge Books and Software

23

Word bank

beautiful

banksias

yummy

wallabies

echidnas

colourful

carefully

ruined

limestone

parrotfish

conger

octopuses

Knowledge Books and Software